Born in the 1950s to a submariner and a 'cockney' rebel, he engaged early with sport and books. A deep thirst for knowledge was well served by King Edward IV Grammar and Royal Holloway College, University of London. Playing a respectable level of football and golf and with a thirty-five-year squash habit, it became apparent that he'd need to work for a living. After a season at Butlin's, cost accounting, grass cutting for the RAF, and an accidental gap year, he stumbled into the brewing trade. Thirty-five years later, after running sales teams across the UK, he set up his own business. An ensuing sense of freedom drew him back to creative writing.

Ronald Charles Mellor
Jean May Mellor, nee Wood
Trevor Andrew Mellor
aka Ma, Pa & Nipper
Ronald Charles Mellor
Jean May Mellor, nee Wood
Trevor Andrew Mellor
aka Ma, Pa & Nipper

Janette, Sean,
Michael, Liz,
Rhys, Ethan, Esme, Lucas
Anthony, Guayarmina,
Eloisa, Mateo
Francesca, DeeJay

Kevin Paul Mellor

RAMBLINGS OF A FREE MAN - VOLUME II

Please join me on my journey

Aug 25

AUSTIN MACAULEY PUBLISHERS®

LONDON · CAMBRIDGE · NEW YORK · SHARJAH

A CIP catalogue record for this title is available from the British Library.

ISBN 9781035889297 (Paperback)
ISBN 9781035889303 (ePub e-book)

www.austinmacauley.com

First Published 2025
Austin Macauley Publishers Ltd®
1 Canada Square
Canary Wharf
London
E14 5AA

Abid Dar—London.
Carl Cullingford—Mallorca.
Christine Allen
Jordan Caulfield
Paul William (M'lud) Reid—North Yorkshire.

Albion—Conwy, Wales.
The Laundry Room—Deganwy, Wales.
Newhall Arms—Cannock, Staffordshire.

Table of Contents

Stambermill 1977   11

Victorian Terrace   13

Bully—Beef or Blokes—Both Unwelcome   15

Oases of Calm   16

Passion   17

Contactless Christopher   18

Forest Find   19

It's Not Compulsory   20

Metrohome West—Midlands Metro   22

Moaner Liza   25

Rhyming Up   26

Dreamland—Reprised   27

Singh—In from High   28

Alleys, Snickets, Ginnels—Definitely Maybe   30

Gravely Told   31

Morning Is Broken   33

Dining a La Trafnidiaeth Cymru (1)   34

Mermaid Mayhem—Conwy Style   36

Alice Ducks the Cooking Class   38

Saints Alive Where Rails Thrive   40

Deganwy Daydream—Summer for the First Time   42

Rapt in Liverpool's Arms   44

Driving Full Circle—Around the Bend   46

Boredom Isn't Boring, Trust Me   47

Blue—Collar Blues   48

Fares Please—Fair or Not   49

HMG to OMG—Initially Simple But…   50

I'm on the Train   52

Stop in the Name of the Lore   53

Stambermill 1977

What did I glimpse that day?
I travelled only to say
I don't know how to pray
That the industry could stay
Shiny sweat against the forge
Most passing by, looking to gorge
On a new life of hope?
Way to clear the acrid smoke
To forget the rhyme of nope
To ignore what went before
To miss why no longer poor
But forged the chains of life
So that we can have no strife.

Victorian Terrace

Are you in there? You must be
I know your bike is outside
Clips on the cross, of course not locked
Ready to go from the very first light.
Still sleeping, I never saw that sight
No need to worry, no need to fight
Shoes and boots from day to night
Keep moving, no cars, must be clocked
Each minute docked, fifteen a guide
Dodge in if not, the foreman doesn't see.

Home by six, food at the table
Keeping all fed from morning to bed
Neighbours work together, stronger that way
Still wearing and carrying military might
This era of work and graft keeps the light
No such challenges lead to flight
This is the adage 'Do the right'
Doesn't matter whether work or play
Doesn't need food to keep the family fed
A submariner, a matelot is always able.

Smoke slides across the street
No heating else, no need to scrimp
Coal waggon, dead wood comes in droves

Chugging the road as a white knight
Dropping into cellars giving a fright
No quarter given, no words a sleight
It's always understood what's wrong or right
Fire blazing, a mother cooking at stoves
Always knitting, always there never skimp
A fifties life, not much but far too fleet.

Bully—Beef or Blokes—Both Unwelcome

Physical threats every day
Probably, usually, they never say
Threats they build, it's not play
Sports, brains it's not their way
No help in the dark of night
Daylight relieves the edge of fright
Too good, not good enough, I care
Just seen again, always there
Brazen it out with the help of friends
Look in the eye, my eye never bends
Someone knows how to deal in law
Clever maybe, not been here before
Let's support everyone in this need
Take these words and put them in your feed.

Oases of Calm

Music bumps the mind, holds court
If only we could stay taut
Or fraught or sought, I thought
What do I know, it will come to nought.

Bump bump, rapping over rap
Never a chance to take a nap
I'm a fan, never call it wrap
Whoever does, it's clearly a trap
Allowing poets, knowing to clap.

Rhyme, rime time and fudge
The slime is mine clearly no judge.

Passion

"Have you ever had a passion fruit martini?"
"I've never had a passion fruit martini."
"Would you like to try a passion fruit martini?"
"I'd love to try a passion fruit martini."
"But have you ever been to Vietnam?"
"Not since the 60s with Uncle Sam."
"No, I mean touring the leafy coast."
"Just a way, I suppose, to make a boast."

"She did this, he did that." And we
Let's face it, I thought he'd see
That we can always use the premise
To speak loudly in public is not remiss
"I'd imagine that most of my fellows
Have not seen or been," he bellows.

Perhaps a touch of self—awareness
Would help us all to feel stressless
Still on he goes, Thos Cook is alive
Off next stop, thankfully, we survive.

Contactless Christopher

Why cash when you can flash the plastic
Keep your seat, wave it, be bombastic
I'm rich, actually, I'm Chris, I think
Always looking for the slightest chink
The one that allows me not to sink
The one that floats in an eye's blink.

But still, who cares, only those who judge
Mean streets, don't mind, never fudge
But still, there's tomorrow, I'll tot it up
Worth it, perhaps one day, still but…

Forest Find

I can't wait
I know it ain't
Nothing but fate
I don't want to wait
It ain't feint
Nor fraught
Not bought
It'll come to naught
It's because
I can wait…so?
It's a date…so?
Call me mate
Straight…so
As they say in Landon
Plenty is often random
A throwaway poem
Is always a theorem.

It's Not Compulsory

To eat on the train especially cheese and onion
To walk on the right to save the bunions
To leave the lock gate closed upwards
To jump an orange light downwards
To vape in a corner, all smoke and chew
To puff post drawing a goth tattoo
To sniff in time despite no cold
To cough no cover, never to be told.
To heroically collect the dog's output in trees
To hog the bar, high stools knocking knees
To recline mid—morning on so short a flight
To buy a daily coffee aloft as a torchlight
To gawp at mobile whilst moving at pace
To spread on trains across the seat with case
To leave straps a—dangling, not over oneself
To take more than a share of overhead shelf
To neglect one's hygiene on train to home
To fill the drive with thousands of stones that roam
To blow a dozen leaves noisily into the drain
To show no link between sense and brain
To hog the pavement with one's best mate
To cycle on the path at speed despite never late
To proudly display a camera in a helmet
To wince in pain when using a pelmet
To pull out in front not increasing speed

To arrive at the checkout, is it cash I need?
To leave one's rubbish next to the bin at the brim
To discuss private stuff loudly at a whim
To deny doing so even more loudly, please
To leave glasses on the table, it's such a wheeze
To over—converse if not invited to speak
To leave it down or forget to raise the seat
To shop the garage but not move your car
To block the road as electric gates move from ajar
To…be continued…or hopefully not
…Perhaps it is, if so, what?

Metrohome West—Midlands Metro

Dive into the tram, history awaits,
Wolves' locks are the key to the past.
Sudden jolt, yet not actually fast
Middle of the road, no fence, no gates

Pipers playing, a view over the fields.
A right royal lament by Briton's true pub
Still flowing away from the central hub
A priest, a field, with awe he kneels.

Rounding the crescent, no dales, no lox
Bil's town notwithstanding, a park away
Proud Wednesbury, perched high they say,
Watching Bradley become a lane pre clocks.

Tunnelling for a lake, as black as night
Streets of Dartmouth, Lodge and West Brom's Hall
The Holy Trinity, a sign, a town that will thrall,
Guns Village, a name that still gives a fright.

Kenrick's not Eddie though free from thorns
His hands, his keys were always worth,
Not green nor Al, nor Winson a dearth
Our Soho, not yours, London mourns.

A jewel in our crown, no quarter given.
St Paul's, hands off, another of ours
Ditto St Chad, we admire his powers.
Bull again; this time nails not riven.

Keep off Manchester, corporation is Brum
Grand Central is not a New York street.
Our town hall and library, books all neat
Reading to the rhythm of Brindley's drum.

There are only thirty-two ways to reach five.
One more to Edgbaston, all village and cricket
It's stumps so it's time for a return ticket,
Back we go, our metro should always thrive.

Moaner Liza

Take a selfie in the Louvre
Go to the loo for a selfish reason
The former's uncouth, the latter's treason
Put the phone in your pocket and then move.

'Next' website, Emmerdale on the red button
Not disparate or desperate or any…ate
You think that viewing will please your mate?
You'd be wrong, these photos are a put—on.

Selfless selfies in soulless sensibility's name
Mirroring the malaise of modern modes
Hold back, or ban these reflections of codes
The emptiness, collected, disseminated in vain

Rhyming Up

Pick up a Metro on the metro
Never forget reading is retro
Still, friends, even enemies expect though
That you'll always find a way to know.

Should ridiculous always say ridicule
Should different always say diffident
Should light always shine darkly
Should the dark always follow the light?

Always be here, always show the light
Always, maybe never, stand and fight
There comes a time in the passing of light
That Joe Average, another sees only flight

As a plan Z, not generational or alpha
Knowing that better than all is beta
Feeling that flying is more than delta
Hearing this, feeling this, it's a belter.

Dreamland—Reprised

Who is that sleeping in my head
Only waking to seal my bed?
If only I was so well-read
Just shows I'm very easily led.

Okay, dreams have a meaning, yes?
If so, what does this mean? I guess
Moving in the night, like a knight in chess
Now I'm free, it cannot all be stress.

I see it all clearly now as Johnny says
Follow the leader, my dream always plays
Falling, climbing, running every which way
Waking shattered, as if living in a maze

Cluttering, stuttering, uttering nonsense
Talking, fighting, frightening pretence
Now, but not later, will it make any sense
It comes, it goes but no idea whence.

Singh—In from High

Manchester Square? I don't think so
Wallace, Scotland then tower to go,
Armour, ceramics, coffee and tea
Just the space is a wonder to see.

Drifting to ground, something more profound
Ranjit's throne and sword there unbound.
A history of proud service to men
Mughals, Afghans, and East India when
Only inner strength could build unity,
Enemies attacking the people with impunity.

Five rivers flowing to a bitter end.
Many brave battles, certainly no friend
If so, they are trained to fight and offend,
Even if treaties are offered, hands extend.
Basic, loyal, each man can transcend,
No other leader, no man can pretend.

Indus, Kashmir, Lahore all proud
Protecting all people, even a crowd
Celebrating in unity, a purity decided
Standing strong and firm, never divided
Protecting an orchard with thorny trees
No way the Golden Temple will be seized.

If only all destinies could be protected
In reality, it's not more than expected,
Aiming for Khalsa at a cost that's fair,
Not on a wing, a hope but through prayer.

Alleys, Snickets, Ginnels—
Definitely Maybe

Owning a cycle or a dog

Even dressing for a jog

Is more saintly than St Chad

But it's me, not them that's bad.

Why do I see through this prism?

Sucking the joy, heading for prison?

Not always a saint, but rarely godless

Rambling sometimes is a holy mess.

Gravely Told

Robert's grave sits gravely in Deia

Deia's delight lit layer by layer

His insights, his life only touches

The poet in me and in your clutches

Words of magic, magic bound in words

But pecking now at the stony ground are birds.

Morning Is Broken

A morning has broken, so they say,
Children dragging, too weary to play,
Still, the walls await, targets drawn,
Mobiles aside, bags too; papers worn.
It's a friend, not an enemy at both gates,
Used to fight but now, all mates.

At nine each day, they face their fates,
Do our best, but let's ignore all traits.
Pass this, learn that don't even think it,
Walk together, talk together, no trinket
Or eyeliners, lipstick, or colours at all
Treating all as individuals will surely appal.

Still, heads down, or up, or what we say
You'll leave here, more will arrive one day.
Tick this box, that form, it forbids play
Your result is not yours, but we're having our way.

Dining a La Trafnidiaeth Cymru (1)

"I don't take it, black pudding that is."
"It's not on the menu, sir." No need to dis
"Black pepper, please?" No eggs are complete
"Mine's Tabasco." Caribbean brunch replete.
If people are now customers, we must be mindful
Albeit many forget it's essentially respectful.

Watching the time, not moving but it does
Wind—whipping stinky—bob just because
The estuary drains, imperceptible to all
Except for the godwit and sandpiper's call.

Do we sway with the wind and the tide
Do Dynion (2) and Menywod (3) the moon abide
"Last call for Llandudno," she chirpily explains
All change, no change, only our Welsh trains.

1-Transport for Wales
2-Men
3-Women

Mermaid Mayhem—Conwy Style

She started to glide along the tide one day
The elders said, "She must stay on land and play."
Edward was too busy building his hearty castle
Her plight, to him and the town, was too much hassle.
Lapwings soaring over the lush tree mallow
To care for her, only knowingly shallow
Okay, fair enough, you'll never make a nurse
I'll struggle and may die but never will this curse.

Alice Ducks the Cooking Class

Did Alice appear from the pier?
Did Charles spy her walking the boards?
No doubt thinking he was lucky to see her.
Short story, novel, or set it to chords?

Summer wonderland shines soulfully bright
A glass to peer through, however dark
Swaying on the tide, eaglets take flight,
The moment captured in history, clear but stark.

Punch glares at Judy, violence forbidden,
The white rabbit despairs the modern script,
Through the glass, he looks almost hidden
Children roar, innocence is fully gripped.

The tide waits for no man or woman too,
History follows history, as Alice knew.

Saints Alive Where Rails Thrive

Paddington barely knew his station,
Padding across the city at night
No wonder he did not see the Black Friar
It would make a King Cross
Especially as Waterloo reprised might fright,
Firing its cannon twinned like pliers.

Only Mary can be this good, as well as proud,
Piano tinkling, ivories glistening but loud.
Two streets apart, Liverpool and the Fens,
Euston's tone deaf, its ifs and whens
Only the design, all Victorian class
Thanks to the poet saving St Pancras

Deganwy Daydream—Summer for the First Time

Was that clickety—click or clickety—clack?
Drumming the iron fingers on a rolling track
The only sound piercing the flat calm sea.

As far as I see, the tides are so key
To drawing a long sandy shore, barefooted
Scattered rocks and marram that just cut it
Into sections of people with canine friends,
A golf course linking its tees and bends
Looming over a millpond of the bay.

Edward's ancient walls encircle Conwy
To the north, the Great Orme paternally looks
Over the well—set town, just as in the books
It can't be like this every day, but why?
The clouds on holiday leaving a clear blue sky.

Rapt in Liverpool's Arms

And so, it rained, no cloud five minutes ago
That's the coast for you, a traveller opined,
Just for once, in the interest of the flow
I agree, tugged up my collar, nicely timed.

"Let's take shelter," I told myself but why?
No one's listening and that includes me.
Liverpool Arms, history, warmth, beer, and dry
Too much choice if like me, you like to see
Every experience; local flavours and smells.

Sitting, coat divested, in a snug of ages,
Old sailors, trawlermen and women tells
Of oft—told tales, by voice, not pages
Each window, stool, and table tell a fable.
The window opens, looks across a calm flow
Ships and trade, mixed with all that are able
I can only admire and thank those in the know.

Driving Full Circle—Around the Bend

Where once were trams, now are prams,
Bouncing in health if not in wealth
Not fed from above but by loyal Mams
Just feeling their way through stealth.

Once the whirr of power transferred
The bounce, the jolts, never disturbed,
Driver and conductor, uniforms preferred,
Passengers only chatted, glimpsed and purred,
Over the now historical tramways of Britain
Long scrapped, consigned and history rewritten,
Electric cars are the future, must be smitten.
Who scrapped these beauties should be fritten.

Build with local skills,
Not generated for thrills
For the people
And in the people's interests
Let's forgive the planners, let's hope they rest.

Boredom Isn't Boring, Trust Me

Is it chat, is it to know or tell?
Perhaps a chance to impress.
If that fails, invoke stories from hell
Trousers, suits, Lycra or dress…

Every conversation, an opportunity, alright
Still, if quiet, all is better no doubt
Lights on, sun shining, but not so bright
It's okay, I HEAR you, no need to shout.

Blue—Collar Blues

For the last time

You want, we'll build it,
Pay me and I'll repay you.
Living close, friends closer
Quality output, quality input.

Pass skills down to you and me
Absorbing the detail and the flow
Building a future brick—by—brick
Stone by stone, bolt and screw.

Still, it makes sense, or no sense at all
To raze to the ground
To sell dreams at a debt,
Councils, I assume must bet.

That it will, all turn out right in the end…the end…the end.

Fares Please—Fair or Not

They say it's a long way from cradle to grave
I cannot remember either
But I bet it's true, wrong or neither
Journeying itself is but for the brave.

It looked so clear the other year
Now it's fear as the last stop is near
Not always, not today, perhaps we're
Just looking to fill a hole of worry
Wild thoughts, regrets; Frank in a flurry
Keep close to facts, never curry
Favours or debts, they end in tears.

Just open up if worry nears
Friends, family, strangers or peers
This journey is for real, with no returns.

Perhaps buy a single and save
Dig for happiness, smiling, not grave
It's odd, good, sad and made by turns.

HMG to OMG — Initially Simple But...

Grabbing our land by the hand
Holding tight; happiness or fright?
Good to see on the TV today
That Sir Kier has entered the fray
The common theme is that we pray
The new administration will start to say
That its core brief is far from short.
These words, those ads don't come to naught.

We've watched the conversion from HMG to OMG
Pillars collapsing, now we all can see
The Post Office stamping over their team
Dealing with miners was more than mean.
Of the blood, tainted, we must wean
This driving force to do the opposite of sense
To look back, to consider that whence
The systems, checks and balances are
More fundamental than the ministerial car.

Which exit was used by common sense?
It's easier or luckier to show pretence
Of picking straws with which to tick the box
Setting a stance, taking the hardest of knocks.

But let's look at what success would mean
Difficult because it's rarely seen.
Take the ideal solution and work to base
Set the focus on results, not on waste.
Make it clear that to cover up is to fail
To be transparent isn't just a boat to sail
It's a core necessity as skies darken
Clear, concise, considerate moves harken.

Surely, we cannot swim and sink
Poor standards and cloudy minds just stink
Take the golden standard and plant it
Up there, high, for all to see flowing
In a positive wind blowing from the centre
Underlining our common desire that meant to
Lead and inspire; overwhelm with compassion.

Not for the tick—box but for the nation
Why not accidentally get it right
Or else the pit of pain is out of sight.

I'm on the Train

Has thirty seconds passed so quickly?

I didn't hear that, or did I?
"I'm on the platform, the forecourt, the bus."
We didn't hear that, not us.

I remembered I'd seen that piece in the paper
'Headphones invented' such a caper.
It doesn't make you look more important.
Really it doesn't. I said, "IT DOESN'T Quiet, please!"

It's a tricky concept, I agree, public transport
One more time please, with ease
It's not the office, open plan or not
Even if you agree, desist and then what?
It'll prompt an outbreak of salt and vinegar
A mastication too far, I'll not linger.

Stop in the Name of the Lore

A simile is a smile as wide as a river
An apostrophe won't be a catastrophe if never
Used where it should, a comma all—comer
A colon takes the stomach of an all—round plumber.

Seeking to drain your pipes with brackets
A van on the path just £100 rackets
"How much?" we exclaim, explaining is curt
Ask questions, feel free; the cost will still hurt.

I'll have to dash, parts are én route
"See you in some hours." Still, it sounds cute
Still, I, causing the problem, could not unblock
Nor fix a leaky tap, period, full stop.